Text © 2016 Elisa M. Camara

Illustration ©2016 Jason Breidenbach

All Rights Reserved

ISBN -13: 978-1523805730

ISBN-10: 1523805730

★ PATRIOT PUP ★

Written with love for my three sons
Joe, Sam & Hank
and in honor of our faithful dog, Cami

 = patriotism

noun|pa·tri·ot·ism|\ˈpā-trē-ə-ti-zəm
love for or devotion to ones country

Hi, I'm Hank. I'm watching my uncle. His name is Mecot. He has a big job. He's a Drill Instructor for the United States Marine Corps. He teaches new troops how to protect and defend our country: the United States of America.

They all know him as Sergeant Camara but he's just Uncle Mecot to me. Today they are marching into the forest for overnight survival training.

"Yikes! It looks like a gigantic storm is heading this way!" I exclaim. And there's my Uncle Mecot shouting to his troops, "All right troops, time to get those tents set up quick! It's going to be a bad one and it's rolling in fast!"

Rain is pouring down from the sky and the rumbling thunder is shaking the ground beneath my feet. When I look up, I see bolts of lightning stretching across the dark clouds. Boom! Crack! Rumble! Suddenly, one of the troops screams, "Sgt. Camara, I hear something! I definitely hear something over there. It sounds like an animal crying! It needs our help!"

"I need two of you to come with me now! Bring your gear and let's move!" grumbles Sgt. Camara. Off they march drugging through the pouring rain and booming thunder. The wind is whipping all around them. Trees are swaying back and forth while they dodge the falling branches. They are on a mission to rescue the mysterious whimpering animal.

"Over there Sergeant! Over there!" The flashlight shines right underneath a huge, old oak tree. There… snuggling right beside the tree trunk, nestled on a soaking wet pile of crunched up leaves rests a little shivering puppy. He is curled up like a cinnamon roll. His scattered spots of mud look just as if he's been sprinkled with cinnamon from his head to his paws.

Sergeant Camara reaches into his pocket and pulls out his patriotic bandana. It's just the right size to wipe off the mud soaked puppy and wrap him up. It is covered in red, white, and blue like our American flag. "Here you go little buddy. Let's wipe that mud off your face and take a look at you." Sergeant Camara whispers while making sure not to scare him.

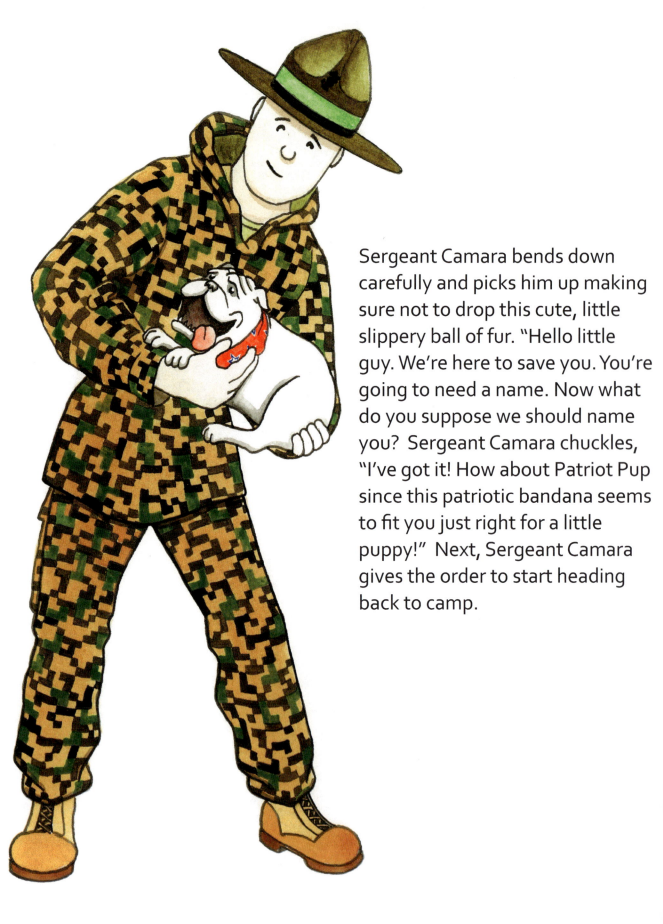

Sergeant Camara bends down carefully and picks him up making sure not to drop this cute, little slippery ball of fur. "Hello little guy. We're here to save you. You're going to need a name. Now what do you suppose we should name you? Sergeant Camara chuckles, "I've got it! How about Patriot Pup since this patriotic bandana seems to fit you just right for a little puppy!" Next, Sergeant Camara gives the order to start heading back to camp.

Suddenly, Sergeant Camara and one of his troops catch a glimpse of something else stirring around that big, old oak tree. He shouts, "Men! Shine the light down here. Come closer!" The beam of light was directed around the other side of the huge tree trunk. In a quiet, quivering voice I say, "Hi Uncle Mecot, it's me."

"Hank, what are you doing out here in this storm getting all soak and wet?" replies Uncle Mecot. I mutter with a grin on my face, "I was thinking it would be an exciting adventure to follow you. But then I heard crying and ended up here instead of camp. Before I could count to ten, I saw you and your troops marching down the riverbank. That's pretty awesome!"

The storm finally passes over and it is the still of the night. No more loud cracks of thunder. No more beating down of rain drops. No more howling wind. Just silence. We are all hiking back to camp one behind the other. We are cold, wet, muddy and tired. When out of nowhere, Patriot Pup leaps out of Uncle Mecot's jacket. Uncle Mecot yells, "Patriot Pup, get back here right now!"

The moonlight is just enough to light up the shadow of a huge, brown bear with big claws and big dark eyes. He is ready to charge at us. Patriot Pup stands fearless. He is ready to protect and defend us.

Although Patriot Pup is a small puppy, he growls the biggest growl I have ever heard, "G-r-r-r-r-r!" The scary bear begins racing towards us. The closer he comes the more I see he is gigantic! He stands on his back legs, claws lurching at us, and he growls right back at Patriot Pup. "G-r-r-r-r-r!" Suddenly the big brown bear stops. He is nose to nose with Patriot Pup. But Patriot Pup stands tough with his paws dug into the ground. He is not going to let that big bear barrel past him.

Patriot Pup lifts his thick head high in the air, staring the bear in the eyes, and growling an even louder, more powerful growl. "G-r-r-r-r-r!" We can hear it echoing off the mountain tops. That bear lowers his enormous head and takes two steps back. The only sound he makes is a little, itty bitty whimper as he slowly begins wandering backwards until he disappears back into the forest.

I nervously shout, "For such a small puppy you sure do let out a big, scary growl, Patriot Pup!" Uncle Mecot picks up Patriot Pup calmly saying, "You saved us Patriot Pup. You protected us from that huge brown bear." I agree, "Hey Uncle Mecot he's just like your troops training to be patriots. He's got an amazing ability to protect and defend us!"

We all begin hiking back to camp. Patriot Pup is marching right beside Uncle Mecot proudly displaying his patriotic bandana.

Patriot Pup ends up sleeping in between Uncle Mecot's sleeping bag and mine. He is curled up, once again, like a little cinnamon roll nestled between the both of us.

As the sun begins to rise over the tops of the trees, we start to break down the tents and pack up the gear. We begin marching back to the Marine Corps Base. Patriot Pup and I march right along with the troops making sure not to step out of line. Uncle Mecot keeps a close eye on both of us making sure we do not wander off on another adventure. Back on base it is time for the lowering of the American flag ceremony. This takes place every evening on military bases throughout our country.

Patriot Pup and I march to the ceremony. Afterwards, Uncle Mecot gives this very special puppy, wearing the patriotic bandana, something very important. It is an official Dog Tag. "What's that?" I ask. Uncle Mecot explains, "It's what we all wear in the military. It has our name and other important information on it. So now Patriot Pup has one with his name on it too! It also has my phone number should he ever get lost." "What about me? Do I get one too?" I mutter. "Of course, Hank," answers Uncle Mecot, "so we don't ever lose you and Patriot Pup on future adventures!"

Patriot Pup is dedicated to Sgt. Mecot Camara who gave his life for our country on 10-23-83. He was the author's only brother. And now his legacy and patriotism will live on through the adventures of his nephew, Hank, and Patriot Pup.

ACKNOWLEDGMENTS

This book would not have been possible without the support and love of the following individuals:

My best friend, Jeff, for your constant encouragement;

My oldest son, Joe, for your incredible editing skills;
My dear friend, Will, for organizing an amazing West Virginia book launch and for keeping me on task;

My dear friend, Cheryl, for getting me through the difficult moments that seemed impossible.
Most especially, to my wonderful family and friends that believed in me and my vision.

Special recognition to The Academy of Learning and the Disabled American Veterans - Chapter 30 in Sanford, Florida for the wonderful book launch and support.

Lastly, thank you so much to my hometown of

Hinton, West Virginia for your endless support and love. Thank you Otter and Oak Outfitter and The Ritz Theater for hosting an outstanding book launch at home.

Patriot Pup Salutes You!

Elisa M Camara was born and raised in West Virginia. She has a degree in Business Administration from Queens University in Charlotte, North Carolina, currently works and lives in Orlando, Florida, and is the mother of three sons.

Jason Breidenbach has been an artist and illustrator since 2005. He has created numerous works of art and illustrations that have been published in magazines, books, and as limited edition prints. He lives in Stafford, VA with his wife and son.

Made in the USA
Charleston, SC
09 February 2016